بِسْمِ اللهِ الرَّحْمٰنِ الرَّحِيْم

رَبِّ يَسِّرْ وَلَا تُعَسِّرْ وَتَمِّمْ بِالْخَيْرِ وَبِكَ نَسْتَعِيْنُ يَا فَتَّاحُ
رَبِّ زِدْنِيْ عِلْمًا

ج	ث	ت	ب	ا
ر	ذ	د	خ	ح
ض	ص	ش	س	ز
ف	ع	ظ	ط	
ن	م	ل	ك	ق
ی	ی	ء	ه	و

رَبِّ يَسِّرْ وَلَا تُعَسِّرْ وَتَمِّمْ بِالْخَيْرِ وَبِكَ نَسْتَعِيْنُ يَا فَتَّاحُ
رَبِّ زِدْنِيْ عِلْمًا

ح	ت	ث	ب	ج
ط	ص	س	ن	ذ
ق	غ	ظ	خ	ض
ع	ل	ش	يـ	ه
م	ي	ن	و	ف
٦	ک	ا	د	ک

ه	س	و	ح	ط	ء	د	ا
ذ	ف	ج	ظ	ب	ن	ك	ص	ع
ث	ي	ش	ق	خ	ز	ض	ت	غ

ج	ص	ث	س	ب	ء	ك	ز	ت
ف	ش	ط	ذ	ل	ض	خ	د	ظ
و	ع	ر	ق	ح	م	ي	ع	ه

ح	ض	ق	ل	ر	ج	م	ع	ث	ت
خ	ب	ذ	ك	ف	ي	ص	ه	ت
ن	ع	ش	ظ	ز	د	س	

ص	ع	ب	ح	ز	ت	ض	ء
ش	ث	ق	ي	غ	خ	ذ	ج	ظ

خ خ	ح ح	ج ج	ث ث	ت ب
ص ص	ش ش	س س	ذ ز	د د
ك ك	ق ق	ف ف	غ ع	ض ض
ي ي	ء ع	ه ه	ن م	ل م

ح	ث ف	خ ص	ب	ئ	ل	غ
ب	ي ض	ت ع	ج ق	د	ن	
غ	ك ص	ش ع	ل	ي	ج	
ض	ق ح	ن ه	ف	ئ ذ	ش	

NOTE : IN LESSON 2 EXPLAIN IN DETAIL THE SHAPES & FORMS OF THE LETTERS.

بس	تر	تم	جل	حج	خط	سد شر
عذ	صب	ضد	غم	فذ	قل	كن لم
ذك	هل	ئذ	ير	ثج	زت	ثب نظ

سبق ۳ — Lesson 3

١	ب	ت	ع	غ	ف
٢	ب بر	پتة تع	عد غ	غ ع	ف ف
ق	ك	ل	م	ه	ي
ق	ك	لالا	مم بہد	ي	ي

مشــق — Exercise

نز	بر	ث	ق	ة	عد	فغة	~	ف	غد	غق
يہ	ت	لا	كل	مة	به	صتة	عہ	ئع	بغ	بغ
نع	بق	بخ	يم	كا	تي	ثي	يي	لي	ني	ني

JOINING UP LETTERS
4

END	MIDDLE	BEGINNING
ا	ـا	ا
ب	ـبـ	بـ
ت	ـتـ	تـ
ة	ـتـ	تـ
ث	ـثـ	ثـ
ج	ـجـ	جـ
ح	ـحـ	حـ
خ	ـخـ	خـ
د	ـد	د

END	MIDDLE	BEGINNING
نذ	ـذ	ذ
ر	ـر	ر
ز	ـز	ز
س	ـسـ	سـ
ش	ـشـ	شـ
ص	ـصـ	صـ
ـض	ـضـ	ضـ
ط	ـطـ	ط
ظ	ـظـ	ظ
ع	ـعـ	ع

EQuranSchool.com

END	MIDDLE	BEGINNING
غ	ـغـ	غـ
ـف	ـفـ	فـ
ـق	ـقـ	قـ
ـك	ـكـ	كـ
ـل	ـلـ	لـ
ـم	ـمـ	مـ
ـن	ـنـ	نـ
ـو	ـو	و
ـه	ـهـ	هـ
ـى	ـيـ	يـ

‍وٌ ـ	‍ـٍ ـ	‍ـً ـ	

دَ	خَ	حَ	جَ	ثَ	تَ	بَ	اَ
طَ	ضَ	صَ	شَ	سَ	زَ	رَ	ذَ
مَ	لَ	كَ	قَ	فَ	عَ	غَ	ظَ
	يَ	ءَ	هَ	وَ	نَ		

جَمَعَ	ثَمَرٌ	بَلَغَ	اَمَرَ
زَعَمَ	رَفَعَ	ذَكَرَ	حَسَدَ
ظَلَمَ	ضَرَبَ	صَدَقَ	سَرَقَ
وَجَدَ	كَسَبَ	قَمَرٌ	عَدَلَ

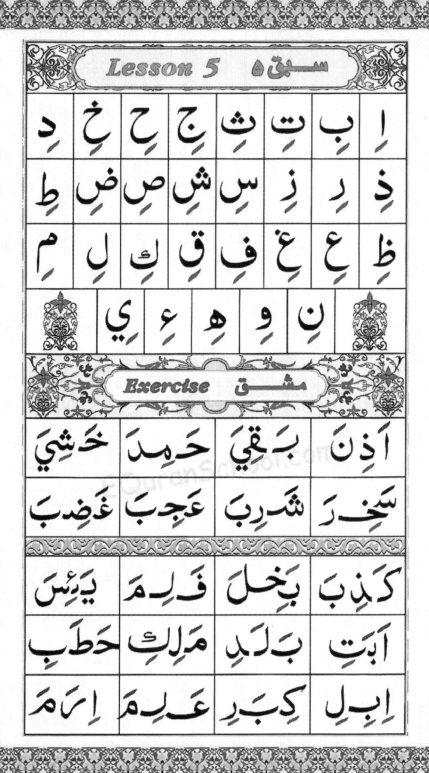

دِ	خِ	حِ	جِ	ثِ	تِ	بِ	اِ
طِ	ضِ	صِ	شِ	سِ	زِ	رِ	ذِ
مِ	لِ	كِ	قِ	فِ	غِ	عِ	ظِ
	يِ	ءِ	هِ	وِ	نِ		

خَشِيَ	حَمِدَ	بَقِيَ	اَذِنَ
غَضِبَ	عَجِبَ	شَرِبَ	سَخِرَ

يَئِسَ	فَهِمَ	بَخِلَ	كَذِبَ
حَطِبَ	مَلِكِ	بَلِدَ	اَبِتَ
اِرَمَ	عَلِمَ	كَبِرِ	اِبِلِ

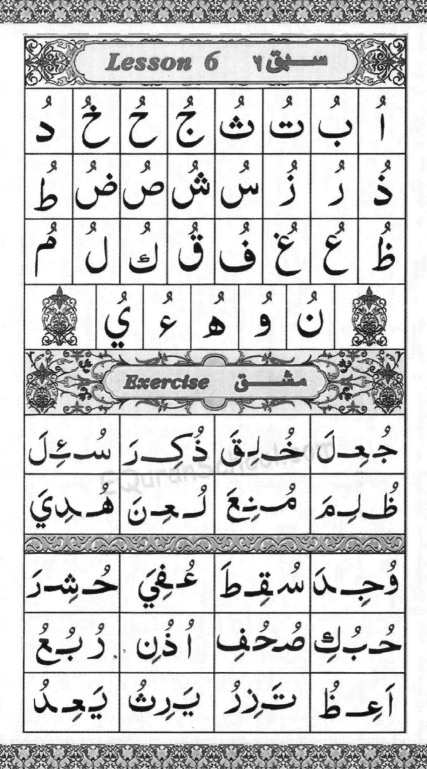

دُ	خُ	حُ	جُ	ثُ	تُ	بُ	اُ
طُ	ضُ	صُ	شُ	سُ	زُ	رُ	ذُ
مُ	لُ	كُ	قُ	فُ	غُ	عُ	ظُ
	يُ	ءُ	هُ	وُ	نُ		

مشق Exercise

سُئِلَ	ذُكِرَ	خُلِقَ	جُعِلَ
هُدِيَ	لُعِنَ	مُنِعَ	ظُلِمَ

حُشِرَ	عُفِيَ	سُقِطَ	وُجِدَ
رُبُعُ	اُذُن	صُحُفٍ	حُبِّكَ
يَعِدُ	يَرِثُ	تَرزُ	اَعِظُ

مَعَ	لِمَ	تَرَ	بِكَ	هِيَ	لَكَ	هُوَ
قَدَرَ	كَسَبَ	حَسَدَ	وَقَبَ	خَلَقَ		
وَلَدَ	فَرَضَ	شَرَحَ	صَدَقَ	وَهَبَ		

غُفِرَ	خُلِقَ	نُفِخَ	هُدِيَ	قُدِرَ		
قُضِيَ	يَضَعُ	كُتِبَ	وُعِدَ	ضُرِبَ		
غَشِيَ	بَخِلَ	نَسِيَ	سَمِعَ	رَضِيَ		

تَبِعَ	يَدِيَ	لَقِيَ	وَلِيَ	لَبِثَ		
رُسُلُ	أُفُقِ	عُقَدِ	أُخَرَ	لَهُوَ		
بِيَدِكَ	خَلَقَكَ	عَدَلَكَ	وَجَدَكَ			

(◌ٗ)	(◌ٖ)	(◌ٓ)

اٰ	بَا	تَا	ثَا	جَا	حَا	خَا	دَا
ذَا	رَا	زَا	سَا	شَا	صَا	ضَا	طَا
ظَا	عَا	غَا	فَا	قَا	كَا	لَا	مَا
	نَا	وَا	هَا	ئَا	يَا		

مشق Exercise

أَبَدًا	رَغَدًا	طَبَقًا	جَنَفًا	مَلِكًا
مَثَلًا	عِنَبًا	قَصَصًا	لَعِبًا	ثَمَنًا
أَسَفًا	قَدَرًا	لَبَنًا	كَذِبًا	شَطَطًا
كُفُوًا	لُبَدًا	سُرُرًا	هُزُوًا	رُسُلًا
عَلَقَةٌ	بَقَرَةٌ	حَسَنَةٌ	نَخِرَةٌ	

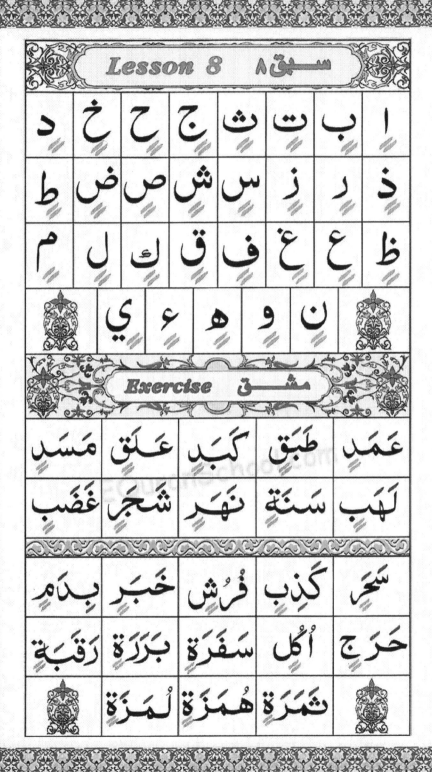

| د | خ | ح | ج | ث | ت | ب | ا |

| ط | ض | ص | ش | س | ز | ر | ذ |

| م | ل | ك | ق | ف | غ | ع | ظ |

| | ي | ء | ه | و | ن | | |

مشق Exercise

| عَمَد | طَبَق | كَبَد | عَلَق | مَسَد |

| لَهَب | سَنَة | نَهَر | شَجَر | غَضَب |

| سَحَر | كَذِب | قُرَش | خَبَر | بِدَم |

| حَرَج | أُكُل | سَفَرَة | بَرَرَة | رَقَبَة |

| ثَمَرَة | هُمَزَة | لُمَزَة | | |

دُ	خُ	حُ	جُ	ثُ	تُ	بُ	اُ
طُ	ضُ	صُ	شُ	سُ	نُ	رُ	ذُ
مُ	لُ	كُ	قُ	فُ	غُ	عُ	ظُ
	يُ	ءُ	هُ	وُ	نُ		

رَجُلٌ	رُسُلٌ	كُتُبٌ	اُذُنٌ	سُرُرٌ
سِنَةٌ	بَشَرٌ	قَسَمٌ	اَحَدٌ	جُلَّدٌ
وَلَدٌ	حُرُمٌ	لَعِبٌ	حَرَجٌ	مَرَضٌ
	بَقَرَةٌ	شَجَرَةٌ	قَتَرَةٌ	غَبَرَةٌ

زَا	رَا	ذَا	خَا	حَا	جَا	ثَا	تَا	بَا
قَا	فَا	غَا	عَا	ظَا	طَا	ضَا	صَا	شَا	سَا
	يَا	ئَا	هَا	وَا	نَا	مَا	لَا	كَا

تَابَ	رَانَ	قَالَ	كَانَ	خَافَ	ذَاتَ
ثَوَابًا	عَامِرٌ	مَالَكَ	هَادٍ	نَارًا	عَادٌ
كَوَاعِبَ	جُنَاحَ	أَصَابَ	يَخَافُ	أَفَاقَ	

غَاسِقٍ	كَاتِبٌ	ثُبَاتٍ	خَالِدًا	جَاعِلٌ	
صَوَابًا	مُطَاعٍ	حَافِظٌ	دَافِقٍ	عَابِدٌ	
أَنَامِلَ	مَوَاخِرَ	رَوَاسِي	فَوَاكِهَ		

١	١ ـ	ـ ٦

خَ	حَ	حَ	جَ	جَ	تَ	بَ	بَ	١	أ
يَ	وَ	مُ	رُ	قُ	فَ	عُ	ظَ	ضَ	شُ	سَ	ذُ

اَلۡ	اٰدَمَ	اٰمَنَ	ذٰلِكَ	اَثَرَ	اٰخَرَ
سَلَمَ	حَلَالًا	مَاۤبًا	کُتُبٌ	مَهۡدًا	اِلٰهَ
اٰیٰتِ	اٰثِرَ	خَلَقۡتِكَ	رِسۡلَتِ	کَلِمَتِ	
قَنِتَتٌ	حَفِظَتٌ	سَمٰوٰتٌ	کُشِفَتۡ		

اِ	ہِ	یِ	ہٖ	یٖ
وُ	ہُ	وُ	ہٗ	ہٗ

اَلِف	هٰذِهٖ	اٰیٰتِهٖ	بِیَدِهٖ	صَاحِبَتِهٖ	
یَرَهٗ	وُہُرِيَ	کُتُبَهٗ	غَاۇنُ	دَاوُدَ	

{ ـــ د }	{ ـــ ـش }

دُوْ	خُوْ	جُوْ	ثُوْ	تُوْ	بُوْ	اَوْ
طُوْ	ضُوْ	صُوْ	شَوْ	سَوْ	نُوْ	رَوْ	ذَوْ
مَوْ	لَوْ	گُوْ	قُوْ	فُوْ	غَوْ	عَوْ	ظُوْ
✿	يُوْ	ءُوْ	هَوْ	وُوْ	نَوْ	✿

مشـــق Exercise

| رَوْحٌ | خَوْفٌ | حَوْلَ | تَوْبَةَ | اَوْهَنَ |
| يَقُوْمِ | فَوْتَ | غُوْرًا | سَوْفَ | نَرُوْجًا |

هَوْنَا	نَوْمٌ	مَوْتِهَا	لَوْمَةَ	كَوْثَرَ
عَفُوْنَا	اَوْتَادًا	يَوْمَئِذٍ	يَرَوْنَهَا	يَوْمَ
صَوْمًا	لَوْحٌ	قَوْلٌ	سَوْطَ	✿

دُوْ	خُوْ	حُوْ	جُوْ	ثُوْ	تُوْ	بُوْ	اُوْ
طُوْ	ضُوْ	صُوْ	شُوْ	سُوْ	زُوْ	رُوْ	ذُوْ
مُوْ	لُوْ	كُوْ	قُوْ	فُوْ	غُوْ	عُوْ	ظُوْ

نُوْ	وُوْ	هُوْ	ءُوْ	يُوْ

مشق Exercise

حُوْرُ	وُجُوْهٌ	تُوْرُوْنَ	بُوْرِكَ	اُوْتِيَ
صُوَرٌ	يَسُوْمُوْنَ	نُوْرًا	لَذُوْ	دُوْلَةً

تَكُوْنُ	يَقُوْلُوْنَ	تَفُوْرُ	اَعُوْذُ	وَطُوْرِ
سَاهُوْنَ	صَائِبُوْنَ	نُوْحٌ	مَوْقُوْفُوْنَ	
ثُبُوْرًا	تَعُوْدُ	شُهُوْدٌ	قُلُوْبٌ	يُوْفُوْنَ

دَيْ	خِيْ	جِيْ	جَيْ	ثُيْ	تِيْ	بِيْ	اَيْ
طَيْ	ضَيْ	صَيْ	شَيْ	سَيْ	زَيْ	رَيْ	ذَيْ
مِيْ	لَيْ	كَيْ	قَيْ	فَيْ	غُيْ	عِيْ	ظَيْ

نِيْ	وَيْ	هَيْ	ئِيْ	يِيْ

مشق Exercise

اَيْنَ	بَيْت	اٰتَيْنَا	حَيْثُ	خَيْرٌ	بِدَيْن

قُرَيْش	زَيْتُوْن	شَيْءٍ	صَيْف	ضَيْف

طَيْرًا	عَيْنٌ	غَيْرَ	كَيْدًا	يَلَيْت	مَيْتًا

وَيْلٌ	بَنَيْنَا	ضَيِّق	رَيْب	لَيْسَ

هَدَيْنَا	هَيْهَات	عَيْنَيْن	بَيْنَهُمَا

دِي	خِي	جِي	جِ	تِي	رِتي	بِي	اِي
طِي	ضِي	صِي	شِي	سِي	زِي	رِي	ذِي
مِي	لِي	كِي	قِي	فِي	غِي	عِي	ظِي
	بِي	ءِي	هِي	وِي	نِي		

اِيتُونِي	مُبِين	يَتِيمًا	كَثِيرًا	مَجِيدُ
مُحِيطُ	اَخِيهِ	نَذِيرُ	كَرِيمُ	تَجْزِى

يَسِيرًا	يَمْشِى	بَصِيرًا	لَطِيفُ	عَظِيمُ
عِينُ	وَغِيضَ	وَقِيلَ	اَكِيدُ	عَلِيمُ
مِيقَاتًا	بَنِيهِ	اٰوِي	شَهِيدُ	لَبِثِين

Lesson 17 سبق ١٧

دَعْ	خُذْ	تُبْ	بَلْ	اِنْ	اَمْ	اِذْ	اَنْ
عِدْ	عَنْ	فَصَّ	سَلْ	زِدْنِي	ذَرْنِي	ذُقْ
كُلْ	كُنْ	لَكُمْ	كَمْ	قُمْ	قُلْ	قَدْ	وَعِظْ
لَهُمْ	فَهْلْ	لِي	هَبْ	مِنْ	مَنْ	لَنْ	كَمْ

Exercise مشق

اَلْقَتْ	اَمْهِلْ	اَنْزِلْ	اِذْهَبْ	اِدْفَعْ
اَحْسِنْ	اُرْكُضْ	اِصْبِرْ	اَمْسِكْ	اَتِمِمْ

قُلْتُمْ	زِلْتُمْ	تَسْمَعْ	يَغْفِرُ
يُعَظِّمْ	اَقْتُلْ	يُدْخِلْكُمْ	
نَقْصُصْ	لَكُنْتُمْ	طِبْتُمْ	

ضَيْفِي	كَيْدِي	دِيْنِي	رُوْحِي	اَيْدِي	قَوْمِي
يَعْفُو	نَبْلُوْكُمْ	تَتْلُوْ	يَرْجُو	تَدْعُوْ	
نَحْنُ	بَعْدُ	بَطْشَ	لَسْتَ	اَنْتَ	
رَفَعْنَا	اَلْهَمَّ	نَعْبُدُ	اَرْسَلَ	اَخْرَجَ	
فَرَغْتَ	اَغْطَشَ	يُوَسْوِسُ		يَحْسَبُ	
اَنْزَلْنٰهُ	اَعْطَيْنٰكَ	اَنْعَمْتَ		اَلْحَمْدُ	
يَشْرَبُ	اُقْسِمُ	تَعْرِفُ	تَرْهَقُ	يَشْهَدُ	
بِاَذِنٍ	وَسْطَنَ	اَثَرْنَ	سُطِحَتْ	نُصِبَتْ	
يَنْظُرُوْنَ	يَسْتَوْفُوْنَ		سَيَعْلَمُوْنَ		

خُسْر	عَدْنٍ	فَصْلٌ	حَبْلٌ	أَجْرُ
تَضْلِيْل	مُقَرَّبَةٌ	مَتْرَبَةٌ	مَسْغَبَةٌ	
مَرْفُوْعَةٌ	تَكْذِيْب	تَقْوِيْم	صِدْق	

نَقْعًا	صُبْحًا	قَدْحًا	مَجْنُوْن	مَشْهُوْد
أَفْوَاجًا	أَتْرَابًا	أَعْنَابًا	أَشْتَاتًا	ٱلْبَابَا

أَغْنٰى	فَهَدٰى	اٰوٰى	اِلٰى	عَلٰى
مِنَ الْأُوْلٰى	وَأَنَا	مِائَةٌ	تَرْضٰى	يَحْيٰى
بِالْغَيْبِ	مَا الْقَارِعَةُ	اٰمَنُوْا		رَضُوْا

NOTE : IN LESSON 18 EXPLAIN THE LETTERS THAT SHOULD NOT BE READ/ PRONOUNCED.

اُولٰٓئِكَ	هٰٓؤُلَآءِ	فَانْصَبْ	وَانْحَرْ اَنَا
بُشْرُ	طُوًى	هُدًى صَلٰوةٌ	زَكٰوةٌ
مُوْصَدَةٌ	شَاْنٌ	يَاْمُرُكُمْ	يُؤْمِنُ
تُؤْثِرُوْنَ		تَاْكُلُوْنَ	يُؤْتُوْنَ

سبق ۱۹ Lesson 19

يَاْتِكُمْ	وَاْمُرْ تَاْتِيْهِمْ	مَاوٰىهُمْ	كَاْسًا
يَاْبَ	نَاْتِ قَرَاْتِ	بَاْسٍ	مَاْكُوْلٌ

فَخُذُوْهُ وَمَا نَهٰىكُمْ عَنْهُ فَانْتَهُوْا
وَاِذْ قَالَ اِبْرَاهِيْمُ لِاَبِيْهِ اٰزَرَ

NOTE : EXPLAIN HOW THE HAMZA WITH A JAZAM ON TOP SHOULD BE READ.
THE ALIF WHICH HAS A JAZAM ON TOP IS KNOWN AS A HAMZA AND SHOULD
BE READ WITH A SLIGHT TWITCH.

ثُمْ مَ=ثُمّ	اِنْ نَ=اِنّ	رَبْ بْ=رَبّ

اَنَّ	حَجَّ	قَلَّ	مَدَّ	مَنَّ	ثُمَّ	عَمَّ

صَلِّ	شَرِّ	اَيِّ	مِمَّ	صَبَّ	ظَنَّ	تَبَّ
حِلٌّ	حَقٌّ	صَفًّا	شَقًّا	دَكًّا	جَمًّا	حُبًّا
ضُرٌّ	ظِلٌّ	غِلٌّ	غَمَّ	رَبُّ	كُلٌّ	اُمٌّ

اِنَّا	مِنَّا	اِيَّاكَ	اِلَّا	كَلَّا	بَلَّا	اَلَّا
اَتِّي	رَبِّي	اِنِّي	مِنِّي	عَنِّي	حَتّى	اَنِّي

اَناسِيَّ	زَكّها	جَلّها	صَلّى	نَشْتّى

يُقَدِّرُ	اَيُّها	اِنَّما	فَلَمَّا	رَبَّنا	اللهُ

عَلَّمَ	وَدَعَكَ	كَذَّبَ	قَدَّرَ	صَدَّقَ
هَمَّت	تَبَّت	ثُوِّب	مِلَّةً	حَصَّلَ
فِيهِنَّ	لَعَلَّ	اِنَّهَا	كُنَّا	اِنَّمَا

عُطِّلَت	زُوِّجَت	كَذَّبَت	تَقَبَّل
يَفِرُّ	يَحُضُّ	يَظُنُّ	يَدُعُّ	يَمُدُّ
نُقَدِّس	نُيَسِّر	تَحَدَّث	يُكَذِّب

مُصَلِّين	بِاَنَّهُم	مُتِمُّ	يُبَيِّن	يَخْتَصُّ
حُقَّت	مُدَّت	خَفَّت	مُنفَكِّين	مُتَّقِين
قُوَّةً	جَنَّةٍ	خَنَّاسٍ	وَالنَّاسِ	تَخَلَّت

عِلِّيِّنَ	عَشِيَّةً	قِيمَةٌ	كَرَّةٌ

~ ۲	~ ۱

بِيْ	بُوْ	بَآ	بِيْ	بُوْ	بَا
سِيْ	سُوْ	سَآ	سِيْ	سُوْ	سَا
سُوْءٌ	مَآءَهَا	شَآءَ	سَآءَ	جَآءَ	بَآءَ
جَزَآءٌ	سَوَآءٌ	اَدَآءً	نِسَآءٍ	غُثَآءً	عَطَآءً
اَوْلِيَآءُ	وَرَآءَهٗ	حُنَفَآءَ	دِمَآءَكُمْ	بَلَآءٌ	
خَطِيْئَتُهٗ	بَرِىْٓءٌ	يُضِيْٓءُ	سَىٰٓءَ	جِىْٓءَ	

NOTE : WITH EXAMPLES EXPLAIN HOW THE LETTER WITH & WITHOUT A MADD SHOULD BE READ-THE LETTERS WITH A MADD ARE STRETCHED LONGER.

مَلَٰٓئِكَةٌ	يَٰٓـَٔادَمُ	كَبَآئِرُ	لَآ اِلٰهَ اِلَّآ اَنْتَ
جَآءُوكَ	اٰلْـٰٔنَ	اٰلْءَ	بَآءُوا

ضَآلًّا	حَآجَّكَ	دَآبَّةٍ	رَآدُّكَ	خَآصَّةٌ
كَآفَّةٌ	بِضَآرِّهِمْ	تَحٰٓضُّونَ	جَآنٌّ	
اٰمِّيْنَ	ظَآلِّيْنَ	ضَآلِّيْنَ	اللّٰهُ	

عَمَّ	عَمَّا	فِيمَ	فِيمَا	مِمَّ	مِمَّا
كَانَّ	كَانَا	اِنَّ	اِنَّا	ظَنَّ	ظَنَّا

NOTE : IT SHOULD BE EMPHASISED THAT THE ALIF AT THE END OF THE WORD SHOULD BE CLEARLY PRONOUNCED.

تَابًا	قَالَا	كَلَّا	لِيَكُوْنَا	فَقُوْلَا	رَسُوْلًا

اِذْهَبَا	شِئْتُمَا	فَلَا تَقْرَبَا	اَطَاعُوْنَا

رَسُوْلٌ مِّنَ اللّٰهِ	كِتَابٌ مُّبِيْنٌ	خَيْرٌ مِّنْهُ

بِحِجَارَةٍ مِّنْ سِجِّيْلٍ	لَوْحٍ مَّحْفُوْظٍ

صُحُفًا مُّطَهَّرَةً	وَّقُوْلُوْا لَهُمْ قَوْلًا

مَعْرُوْفًا	مَتَاعًا لَّكُمْ	خَيْرٌ لِّاَنْفُسِهِمْ

جَنّٰتٍ لَّهُمْ	زُبَلًا لَّرَابِيًا	غَفُوْرٌ رَّحِيْمٌ

عِيْشَةٍ رَّاضِيَةٍ

لَآ اِلٰهَ اِلَّا اللّٰهُ مُحَمَّدٌ رَّسُوْلُ اللّٰهِ

وَاِنْ مِّنْ شَيْءٍ	مِنْ مِّثْلِهٖ	مِنْ مَّاءٍ
اَنْ لَّمْ يَرَهٗ	لَمْ يَكُنْ لَّهٗ	مِنْ لَّدُنْهُ
قُلْ	اَنْ رَّاٰهُ	مَنْ رَّحِمَ	مِنْ رَّبِّكَ
عَابِدٌ	بَلْ رَّفَعَ	زِدْنِيْ عِلْمًا	رَّبِّ
وَعَدْتَّهُمْ	وَجَدْتُّمْ	مَّا عَبَدْتُّمْ
وَارْكَبْ مَّعَنَا	كِدْتَّ	وَاِنْ عُدْتُّمْ

اِيْمَانًا	وَّلَا نَصِيْرًا	وَّلِيًّا	حَبًّا وَّنَبَاتًا
مَالٌ وَّلَا بَنُوْنَ	اِلٰهٌ وَّاحِدٌ	وَّقَالُوْا

شَرًّا يَّرَهُ	اَفَمَنْ وَّعَدْنَا	يَوْمَئِذٍ وَّاجِفَةٌ
يَوْمَئِذٍ يَّصَّدَّرُ	وَيْلٌ يَّوْمَئِذٍ	خَيْرًا يَّرَهُ
فَمَنْ	اَنْ يَّشَاءَ	دَافِقٍ يَّخْرُجُ	النَّاسُ
وَاِنْ يُّرِيْدُوْا	اِنْ يَّنْصُرْكُمْ	يَعْمَلْ

ذَنْبٍ	لَيُنْبَذَنَّ	بِالْجَنْبِ	مِنْ بَعْدٍ
اَنْبَتْنَا	مِنْ بَيْنِ	مِنْ بُخْلٍ	اَنْبِيَاءُ
خَبِيْرٌ بِمَا تَعْمَلُوْنَ	لَنَسْفَعًا بِالنَّاصِيَةِ	
سَوَآءٌ بَيْنَنَا	عَلِيْمٌ بِهِ	اَبَدًا بِمَا

قَدِيرُ الَّذِي	لُمَزَةِ الَّذِي	نُوحُ ابْنَهُ
خَيْرًا الْوَصِيَّةُ		شَيْئًا اتَّخَذَهَا

أَعُوذُ بِاللهِ مِنَ الشَّيْطَانِ الرَّجِيمِ ۝

قُلْ هُوَ اللهُ أَحَدٌ ۝ مِنْ خَوْفٍ ۝ وَجَنَّتْ

أَلْفَافًا ۝ إِذَا حَسَدَ ۝ لِمَا يُرِيدُ ۝ بِأَصْحَبِ

الْفِيلِ ۝ أَبِي لَهَبٍ وَّتَبَّ ۝ لِمَنْ خَشِيَ رَبَّهُ ۝

لِتَعْجَلَ بِهِ ۝ إِنَّهُ كَانَ تَوَّابًا ۝ وَشَاهِدٍ وَّ

مَشْهُودٍ ۝ مِنْهُمْ تُقَّةً ۝ ذُرِّيَّةً طَيِّبَةً ۝

NOTE : IT SHOULD BE EXPLAINED TO THE CHILDREN THE WAY IN WHICH ONE SHOULD STOP AT THE END OF THE WORD & THE SOUNDING OF THE LAST LETTER.

أَصْحَابُ الْقَرْيَةِ ۚ تَمَّ سَمْعَ سَمَاوَاتٍ ۖ مَّا الْعَقَبَةُ ۚ

فَاسْتَبِقُوا الْخَيْرَاتِ ۖ وَيُرْبِي الصَّدَقَاتِ ۖ

بِالْوَادِ الْمُقَدَّسِ طُوًى ۖ يَتْبَعُهَا أَذًى ۚ

وَنِسَاءٌ ۚ لَيْسُوا سَوَاءً ۚ أَخَاهُمْ صَالِحًا ۖ

نَارٌ حَامِيَةٌ ۚ كُتُبٌ قَيِّمَةٌ ۚ إِلَّا هُوَ ۖ

أَعْمَالَهُمْ ۖ أَوْحَىٰ لَهَا ۚ مَن دَسَّاهَا ۚ

إِذْ صَلَّىٰ ۚ لَشَتَّىٰ ۚ جَنَّتِي ۚ إِذَا يَسَرَ ۚ

وَتَوَاصَوْا بِالصَّبْرِ ۚ حَتَّىٰ مَطْلَعِ الْفَجْرِ ۚ

أَبَابِيلَ ۚ تَرْمِيهِمْ ۖ أَفْوَاجًا ۖ فَسَبِّحْ ۖ

وَالْفَجْرِ ۚ وَلَيَالٍ ۖ يَوْمَئِذٍ وَاجِفَةٌ ۚ

أَبْصَارُهَا خَاشِعَةٌ ۖ كَيْدًا ۖ وَّأَكِيدُ ۔

فِى الْعُقَدِ ۙ وَالتِّيْنِ ۙ مَا الطَّارِقُ ۙ

النَّجْمُ الثَّاقِبُ ۙ اَمْرٍ ۖ سَلَمٌ ۙ

وَسَلَامٌ عَلَى الْمُرْسَلِيْنَ ۙ

وَالْحَمْدُ لِلّٰهِ رَبِّ الْعَٰلَمِيْنَ ۙ

تَمَّتْ

آلٓمٓ	آلٓمٓصٓ	الٓرٰ	الٓمٓرٰ	كٰهٰيٰعٓصٓ
طٰهٰ	طٰسٓمٓ	طٰسٓ	يٰسٓ	صٓ	حٰمٓ
	حٰمٓ	عٓسٓقٓ	قٓ	نٓ

NOTE : IT IS A VIRTUE TO MEMORISE THE HUROOF-E-MU-QAT-TA-AAT,

SIX KALIMAHS ششکلمه

FIRST KALIMAH TAYYIBAH پہلا کلمہ طیب
(CODE OF UNITY)

لَا اِلٰهَ اِلَّا اللهُ مُحَمَّدٌ رَّسُوْلُ اللهِ ۝

Laa Ilaaha IllAllahu Muhammadur Rasulullaah
There is none worthy of worship besides Allah;
Muhammad ﷺ is the messenger of Allah.

SECOND KALIMAH SHAHAADAT دوسرا کلمہ شہادت
(CODE OF TESTIMONY)

اَشْهَدُ اَنْ لَّا اِلٰهَ اِلَّا اللهُ وَحْدَهٗ لَا شَرِيْكَ لَهٗ
وَاَشْهَدُ اَنَّ مُحَمَّدًا عَبْدُهٗ وَرَسُوْلُهٗ ۝

**Ashhadu allaa ilaaha illal laahu wahdahu laa
shareekalahu wa ashhadu anna Muhammadan
abduhu wa rasuluhu**
I bear witness that there is none worthy of worship besides
Allah. He is alone. He has no partner, and I bear witness
that Muhammad ﷺ is His servant and messenger.

THIRD KALIMAH TAMJEED تیسرا کلمہ تمجید
(CODE OF UNITY OF GLORIFICATION OF ALLAH)

سُبْحَانَ اللهِ وَالْحَمْدُ لِلّٰهِ وَلَا اِلٰهَ اِلَّا اللهُ وَاللهُ اَكْبَرُ
وَلَا حَوْلَ وَلَا قُوَّةَ اِلَّا بِاللهِ الْعَلِيِّ الْعَظِيْمِ ۝

**Subhaanal laahi wal hamdu lillaahi wa laa ilaaha illal
laahu wAllahu akbar wa laa hawla walaa Quwwata
illaaa billaa hil Aliyyil Azeem**
Glory be to Allah, and all praise be to Allah. There is none
worthy of worship besides Allah and Allah is the Greatest.
There is no power and might except from Allah,
The Most High, The Great.

FOURTH KALIMAH TAUHEED
(CODE OF UNITY OF ONENESS OF ALLAH)

چوتھا کلمہ توحید

لَا اِلٰهَ اِلَّا اللهُ وَحْدَهُ لَا شَرِيْكَ لَهُ لَهُ الْمُلْكُ وَلَهُ الْحَمْدُ
يُحْيٖ وَيُمِيْتُ وَهُوَ حَيٌّ لَّا يَمُوْتُ اَبَدًا اَبَدًا ذُوالْجَلَالِ
وَالْاِكْرَامِ بِيَدِهِ الْخَيْرُ وَهُوَ عَلٰى كُلِّ شَيْءٍ قَدِيْرٌ

Laa ilaaha illAllahu wahdahu laa shareekalahu
lahul mulku wa lahul hamdu yuhyee wa yumeetu
wa huwa hayyun, la yamuto abadan abada.
Zuljalaale wal Ikraame bi yadihil khair
wa huwa 'alaa kulli shayien qadeer

There is none worthy of worship besides Allah who is
alone. He has no partner. For Him is the Kingdom, and
for Him is all praise. He gives life and causes death. He
is Everlasting, He will never die, He is Majestic and
Benevolent. In His hand is all good. And He has power
over everything.

FIFTH KALIMAH ASTAGHFAR

پنجم کلمہ استغفار

اَسْتَغْفِرُ اللهَ رَبِّيْ مِنْ كُلِّ ذَنْبٍ اَذْنَبْتُهُ عَمَدًا اَوْ خَطَأً سِرًّا
اَوْ عَلَانِيَةً وَّاَتُوْبُ اِلَيْهِ مِنَ الذَّنْبِ الَّذِيْ اَعْلَمُ وَمِنَ الذَّنْبِ الَّذِيْ
لَا اَعْلَمُ اِنَّكَ اَنْتَ عَلَّامُ الْغُيُوْبِ وَسَتَّارُ الْعُيُوْبِ وَغَفَّارُ
الذُّنُوْبِ وَلَا حَوْلَ وَ لَا قُوَّةَ اِلَّا بِاللهِ الْعَلِيِّ الْعَظِيْمِ

Astaghfirullaaha rabbi min kulli zanbin aznabtuhu
'amadan aw khata an sirran aw 'alaaniyyatan wa
atoobu ilaihe minaz zanbil lazi a'alamu wa minaz
zambil lazi la a'alamu innaka anta allaamul gyoobi
wa sattaarul 'uyoobi wa ghaffaruz zunoobi wa laa
hawla walaa Quwwata illaa billaahil 'Aliyyil Azeem

I seek forgiveness from Allah, my Lord, for every sin I have committed deliberately or in error, secretly or in public. And I repent before Him for the sin I know of and for the sin I do not know of Indeed! You are the Knower of the thing unseen, and the Councillor of shortcomings and the Forgiver of sins, And there is no power and might except from Allah, the Most High, the Great.

SIXTH KALIMAH RADDE KUFR ششم کلمہ رد کفر

(CODE OF NULLIFICATION OF DISBELIEF)

اَللّٰهُمَّ اِنِّیْ اَعُوْذُ بِكَ مِنْ اَنْ اُشْرِكَ بِكَ شَيْئًا
وَّاَنَا اَعْلَمُ بِهٖ وَاَسْتَغْفِرُكَ لِمَا لَآ اَعْلَمُ بِهٖ تُبْتُ عَنْهُ وَ
تَبَرَّأْتُ مِنَ الْكُفْرِ وَالشِّرْكِ وَالْكِذْبِ وَالْغِيْبَةِ وَالْبِدْ
عَةِ وَالنَّمِيْمَةِ وَالْفَوَاحِشِ وَالْبُهْتَانِ وَالْمَعَاصِىْ كُلِّهَا
وَاَسْلَمْتُ وَاَقُوْلُ لَآ اِلٰهَ اِلَّا اللهُ مُحَمَّدٌ رَّسُوْلُ اللهِ

Allah humma innee a'oozu bika min an ushrika bika shay'awn wa ana a'alamu bihi wa astaghfiruka limaa laa a'alamu bihi tubtu 'anhu wa tabarratu minal kufri wash shirki wal kizbi wal ghibate wal bidate wal namimate wal fawahishe wal buhtaane wal ma'aasi kullihaa wa aslamtu wa aqulu laa Ilaaha illal laahu Muhammadur Rasulullah

O Allah, Surely I do seek refuge in You from knowingly associating any partner with You knowingly; I beg Your forgiveness for the sin from which I am not aware of; I repent it and I declare myself free of infidelity, polytheism (associating any partner with Allah) telling lies and all other sins. I accept Islaam and believe and declare that there is none worthy of worship besides Allah and Muhammad ﷺ is the messenger of Allah.

IMAANE MUFASSAL

(ARTICLES FAITH)

اٰمَنْتُ بِاللهِ وَمَلَآئِكَتِهٖ وَكُتُبِهٖ وَرُسُلِهٖ وَالْيَوْمِ الْاٰخِرِ وَالْقَدْرِ خَيْرِهٖ وَشَرِّهٖ مِنَ اللهِ تَعَالٰى وَالْبَعْثِ بَعْدَ الْمَوْتِ۰

Aamantu billaahi wa malaa'ikatihi wa kutubihi
wa rusulihi wal yawmil aakhiri wal qadri khairihi
wa sharrihi minal laahi ta, aala wal ba'athi
b'adal mawt.

I believe in Allah and in His Angels and in His books
and in His Messengers and in the last day and in fate
that everything, good or bad is decided by Allah,
the Almighty and in the life after death.

IMAANE MUJMAL

(FAITH CONCISE FORM)

اٰمَنْتُ بِاللهِ كَمَا هُوَ بِاَسْمَآئِهٖ وَصِفَاتِهٖ وَقَبِلْتُ جَمِيْعَ اَحْكَامِهٖ اِقْرَارٌ بِاللِّسَانِ وَتَصْدِيْقٌ بِالْقَلْبِ۰

Aamantu billaahi kamaa huwa bi asmaa'ihi wa
sifaatihi wa qabiltu jamee'a ahkaamihi. Iqrarun
bil-lisani wa tasdiqum bilqalbi.

I believe in Allah (as He is) with all His names and
Attributes and I accept all His commands. I accept
verbally and endorse this truth from core of my heart.

TASBIHAT-I-SALAAT

THANA ثناء

سُبْحٰنَكَ اللّٰهُمَّ وَبِحَمْدِكَ وَتَبَارَكَ اسْمُكَ وَتَعَالٰى جَدُّكَ وَلَا اِلٰهَ غَيْرُكَ ۰

Subhanak allahumma wa bihamdika
wa tabarakasmuka wa ta'ala jadduka wa lailaha
ghairuka
All Glory be to you O Allah! and praise be to you;
Blessed is Your name and Exalted is Your Majesty,
and there is none worthy of worship besides You.

RUKU ركوع

سُبْحَانَ رَبِّيَ الْعَظِيمِ ۰

Subhana rabbiyal azîme
How Glorious is my Lord the Great!

TASMEE تسميع

سَمِعَ اللّٰهُ لِمَنْ حَمِدَهُ ۰

Sami-allahu liman hamidah
Allah has listened to him who has praised Him.

TAHMEED تحميد

رَبَّنَالَكَ الْحَمْدُ ۰

Rab-ba-naa la-kal hamd.
O Our Lord! Praise be to You.

SAJDAH سجده

سُبْحَانَ رَبِّيَ الْأَعْلٰى ۰

Subhana ribbiyal a'ala
All Glory be to my Lord, the Highest of all.

TASHAHHUD

الْتَحِيَّاتُ لِلّٰهِ وَالصَّلَوٰتُ وَالطَّيِّبٰتُ السَّلَامُ عَلَيْكَ اَيُّهَا النَّبِىُّ
وَ رَحْمَةُ اللّٰهِ وَبَرَكَاتُهُ السَّلَامُ عَلَيْنَا وَعَلٰى عِبَادِ اللّٰهِ
الصَّالِحِيْنَ ○ اَشْهَدُ اَنْ لَّا اِلٰهَ اِلَّا اللّٰهُ وَ اَشْهَدُ اَنَّ مُحَمَّدًا
عَبْدُهٗ وَرَسُوْلُهٗ ○

At-tahiyatu lillahi was-salawatu wat-taiyibatu
as salamu 'alaika aiyohan-nabio wa rahmatul-lahi
wa barakatuhu as-salamu alina wa'ala ibadillahis-
salihin, ashhadual-lailaha illallahu wa ashhadu
anna muhammadan abduhu warasuluhu.

All reverence, all worship, all sanctity are due to Allah
Peace be upon you O Prophet! And the Mercy of Allah
and His Blessings. Peace be upon us and all the
righteous servants of Allah. I bear witness that none is
worthy of worship besides Allah and Muhammad ﷺ
is His devotee and Messenger.

DUROOD SHAREEF

اَللّٰهُمَّ صَلِّ عَلٰى مُحَمَّدٍ وَّعَلٰى اٰلِ مُحَمَّدٍ كَمَا صَلَّيْتَ
عَلٰى اِبْرٰهِيْمَ وَعَلٰى اٰلِ اِبْرٰهِيْمَ اِنَّكَ حَمِيْدٌ مَّجِيْدٌ ○

Allahumma Salli'ala Muhammadin wa'ala aali
Muhammadin kama sllaita'ala ibrahima wa'ala
aali ibrahima innaka hamidum majid.

O Allah! Shower Your mercy upon Muhammad ﷺ and
the followers of Muhammad ﷺ as You showered Your
mercy upon Ibraheem عليه السلام and the followers of
Ibraheem عليه السلام Verily, You are praiseworthy, glorious.

اَللّٰهُمَّ بَارِكْ عَلٰى مُحَمَّدٍ وَّعَلٰى اٰلِ مُحَمَّدٍ كَمَا بَارَكْتَ عَلٰى اِبْرَاهِيْمَ وَعَلٰى اٰلِ اِبْرَاهِيْمَ اِنَّكَ حَمِيْدٌ مَّجِيْدٌ ۰

Allahumma barik 'ala muhammadin wa ala aali muhammadin. kama barakta ala ibrahima wa'ala aali ibrahima innaka hamidum majid.

O Allah! Shower Your mercy upon Muhammadﷺ and the followers of Muhammadﷺ as You showered Your mercy upon Ibraheem۩ and the followers of Ibraheem۩ Verily, You are praiseworthy, glorious.

THE DU'A AFTER DUROOD درود شریف کے بعد کی دعا

رَبِّ اجْعَلْنِيْ مُقِيْمَ الصَّلٰوةِ وَمِنْ ذُرِّيَّتِيْ ۥ رَبَّنَا وَ تَقَبَّلْ دُعَآءِ ۰ رَبَّنَا اغْفِرْ لِيْ وَلِوَالِدَيَّ وَلِلْمُؤْمِنِيْنَ يَوْمَ يَقُوْمُ الْحِسَابُ ۰

Rabbij-Alni muqimas-salate wa min zurriyati, Rabbana wa taqabbal dua. Rabbanagh firli Wa liwalidayya wa lil mu'mineena yauma yaqoomul hisab.

Our Lord! Make me and my children steadfast in prayer; Our Lord! Accept the prayer. Our Lord! Forgive me. And my parents and believers on the day of judgement.

SALAAM سلام

اَلسَّلَامُ عَلَيْكُمْ وَرَحْمَةُ اللّٰهِ

As salamo alaikum wa rahmatullah
Peace be upon you and the Mercy of Allah

اَللّٰهُمَّ اِنَّا نَسْتَعِيْنُكَ وَنَسْتَغْفِرُكَ وَنُؤْمِنُ بِكَ وَنَتَوَكَّلُ عَلَيْكَ وَنُثْنِى عَلَيْكَ الْخَيْرَ وَنَشْكُرُكَ وَلَا نَكْفُرُكَ وَنَخْلَعُ وَنَتْرُكُ مَنْ يَّفْجُرُكَ اَللّٰهُمَّ اِيَّاكَ نَعْبُدُ وَلَكَ نُصَلِّى وَنَسْجُدُ وَاِلَيْكَ نَسْعٰى وَنَحْفِدُ وَنَرْجُوْا رَحْمَتَكَ وَنَخْشٰى عَذَابَكَ اِنَّ عَذَابَكَ بِالْكُفَّارِ مُلْحِقٌ ۚ

Allahumma inna nasta'inuka wanastaghfiruka
wanuminu bika wanata wakkalu alaika wa nusni
alaikalkhairu wa nashkuruka wala nakfuruka wa
nakhlau wa natruku main-yafjuruka allahumma
iyyaka na'budu walaka nusalli wa-nasjudu
wa-ilaika nas'a wa-nahfidu wa narju rahmataka
wa nakhsha 'azabaka inna 'azabaka
bil-kuffari mulhiq.

(O Allah! We beseech Your help and we ask Your pardon
and we believe in You, and we put our trust in You and
we praise You in the best manner and we thank You and
we are not ungrateful to You and we cast off and leave
one who disobeys You. O Allah! You alone we serve and
to You do we pray and we prostrate and to You do we
flee and we are quick and we hope for Your mercy and
we fear Your punishment. No doubt Your punishment
overtakes the unbelievers.

THE PROCEDURE OF MAKING WUDHU

1. To wash one's hands, face and feet, etc. before performing NAMAAZ is called WUDHU or ABLUTION. No Namaaz is accepted without Wudhu.

2. One should sit on a high, and clean place to perform Wudhu. Face the direction of the Holy KA'BA Sharif if possible.

DUAA BEFORE COMMENCING WUDHU

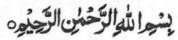

3. Using *Tahir* (clean) water *first* wash *both* the *hands* upto the *wrists three* times.

4. Use a *Miswaak* for cleaning the teeth and then *gargle* the mouth *three* times.

   * It is *Sunnat* to make *Miswaak* during *Wudhu*

5. Thereafter take water upto the *nostrils three* times with the *right* hand and clean the nose with the *left* hand.

6. Then wash your *face three* times. Wash from the hairy part of the forehead to below the chin and from one ear lobe to the other.

7. Then make *Khilal* of the *beard.*

8. Thereafter wash the *right hand including* the *elbows three* times.

9. Then wash the *left hand including* the *elbows* thrice.

10. Then make *Khilal* of the *Fingers.*

11. Thereafter with the hands and pass them over the head, ears and nape. This must be done once only. It is known as *Masah.*

MASAH [wet the hands & fingers] * keep *three* fingers of each hand together (middle finger, ring finger and little finger).* keep thumb and index finger raised (away). *keep thumb, index finger and palm away from the head. Pass the three fingers from the forehead to the upper portion of the nape. * Then place the palm on the sides of the head and bring forward to forehead

* Then insert the front portion of the index finger into the openings of the ear.

* Then make Masah behind the ears with the inner part of the thumb.

* Make Masah of the nape with the back of the middle finger, ring finger and little finger.

12. Then wash *both* the *feet including* the *ankles three* times. First the *right* and then the *left* foot.

* First wash the *right foot* then make *khilal* including the ankle and of the *toes.*
* Then wash the *left foot* then make *khilal* including the ankle and of the *toes.*

PERFORM SALAH CORRECTLY

When you begin the Salah:

1. Make *Niyyah* or intention in your heart to the effect that you are offering such and such *Salah*. It is not necessary to say the words or the *Niyyah* verbally.

2. Raise your hands up to your ears in a way that palms face *Qiblah* and the ends of the thumbs either touch the lobes of the ears or come parallel to them. The rest of the fingers stay straight pointing upwards. There are some who would tend to turn the direction of their palms towards their ears rather than having them face the *Qiblah*.

There are some others who almost cover their ears with their hands. There are still others who would make a faint symbolic gesture without raising their hands fully upto the ears. Some others grip the lobes of their ears with their hands. All these practices are incorrect and contrary to Sunnah. These should be abandoned.

3. While raising your hands in the manner stated above, say: اَللّٰهُ اَکْبَرْ *Allah-akbar.* Then using the thumb and the little finger of your right hand, make a circle round the wrist of your left hand and hold it. You should then spread out the three remaining finger of your. Right hand on the neck of your left hand so that these fingers face the elbow.

4. Placing both hands slightly below the navel, fold them as explained above.

When you are standing:

1. If you are making your *Salaat* alone, or leading it as Imam you first recite *thana'*: سُبْحَنَكَ اللّٰهُمَّ then *Surah al-Fatiha,* then some other *Surah.* If you are behind an Imam, you only recite *Thana:* سُبْحَنَكَ اللّٰهُمَّ and then stand silent listening attentively to the recitation of the Imam. If the Imam's recitation is not loud enough for you to hear, you should be thinking of *Surah al-Fatihah* using your heart and mind without moving your tongue.

2. When you are reciting yourself, it is better that you, while reciting *Surah al-Fatihah,* stop at every verse and break your breath. Recite the next verse in a single breath. For example, break your breath at اَلْحَمْدُ لِلّٰهِ رَبِّ الْعٰلَمِيْنَ ۞ then on الرَّحْمٰنِ الرَّحِيْمِ ۞ then on. مٰلِكِ يَوْمِ الدِّيْنِ ۞ Recite the whole *Surah al-Fatihah* in this manner. But, there is no harm if, during recitation that follows, more than one verse has been recited in a single breath.

3. Do not move any part of your body without the need. In peace the more, the better. If you have to scratch or do something else like that, use only one hand and that too, under very serious compulsion using the least time and effort.

4. Transferring the weight of the body on to one leg and leaving the other weightlessly loose to the limit that it shows a certain bend is against the etiquette of Salaat. Abstain from it. Either you transfer your body weight equally on both legs or if you must channel your body weight on one leg, you have to do it in a way that the other leg shows no bend or curve.

5. If you feel like yawning, try your best to stop it.

6. When standing for *Salaat,* Keep your eyes looking at the spot where you make your *Sajdah.* Abstain from looking to your right and left, or front.

When in Ruku:

When you bend for *Ruku'* watch out for the following.

1. Bend the upper part of your body up to point where the neck and back nearly level up. Do not bend any more less than that.

2. While in *Ruku'* do not bend the neck to the limit that the chin starts touching the chest, nor raise it so high that the neck goes higher than the waist level. Instead, the neck and the waist should be in onelevel.

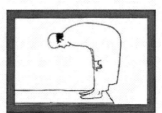

3. In *Ruku;* keep feet straight. Do not place them with an outward or inward slant.

4. Place both hands on your knees in a way that fingers of both hands stay open. In other words, there should be space between every two fingers when you thus go on to hold the right knee with your right hand and left knee with your left hand.

5. In the state of *Ruku,* wrists and arms should remain stretched straight. They should not bend, curve or sag.

6. Stay in *Ruku'* at least for a time during which سُبْحَانَ رَبِّیَ الْعَظِیْمِ could be said three times calmly and comfortably.

7. Stay in *Ruku'* the eyes should be looking towards the feet.

8. Body weight should be evenly distributed on both feet and both knees should be parallel to each other.

Returning to the standing position from Ruku:

1. While returning from *Ruku,* back to the standing position, see that you stand straight leaving no sag or droop in the body.

2. In this position as well, eyes should be fixed on the spot where you do your *Sajdah.*

3. There are those who simply make a 'gesture' of rising from the *Ruku'* instead of rising fully and standing upright when it is time to do so and who, in that very state, when their body is  still bent down Wards, go on their *Sajdah* for them it becomes obligatory that they make their *Salaat* all over again. Therefore, abstain from it very firmly. Unless you make sure about position, do not go for *Sajdah..*

When bowing down for Sajdah:

Remember the following method when bowing down for *Sajdah:*

1. Bending the knees first of all, take them towards the prayer floor in a way that the chest does not lean forward. When the knees have already been rested on the floor, the chest should then be lowered down.

2. Until such time that the knees have come to rest against the floor, abstain, as far as possible, from bending or lowering the upper part of the body.

These days negligence in observing this particular rule of etiquette while getting ready to go for *Sajdah* has become very common. Many people would lower down their chest right from the start and go on to do their *Sajdah.* But, the correct method is what has been stated in #1 and #2 above. Unless it be for a valid reason, this method should not be by passed.

3. After having rested your knees on the floor, place your hands first, then the tip of the nose, then the forehead.

In Sajdah:

1. While in *Sajdah*, keep your head in between your two hands in a way the ends of the two thumbs come parallel to the ear-lobes.

2. In *Sajdah*, fingers on both hands should remain close together, that is, the fingers should adjacent to each other leaving no space in between them.

3. The direction of the fingers should be towards the *Qiblah*.

4. The elbows should stay raised off the floor. It is not correct to rest the elbows on the floor.

5. Both arms should stay apart from armpits and sides. Never keep them tucked in.

6. Do not, at the same time, poke your elbows far out to your right and left causing discomfort to those making *Salah* next to you.

7. The thighs should not come in contact with the stomach wall. The stomach and the thighs should stay apart.

8. During the entire *Sajdah*, the nose-tip should continue to rest on the floor.

9. Both feet should be placed upright on the floor with heels showing on top and all fingers turner turned flat on the floor in the direction of the *Qiblah*. Those who cannot turn all their fingers because of the physical formation of their feet, they will still do well to turn them as much as they can. It is not correct to place the fingers vertically on the floor just for no valid reason.

10. Be careful that your feet do not lift off the floor during *Sajdah*. Some people would do their *Sajdah* while none of the fingers on their feet come to rest on the floor even for a moment. This way the obligation on *Sajdah* is not liquidated at all, and as a result, the *Salaat* too becomes invalid. Be very particular in abstaining from this error.

11. In the stage of *Sajdah,* the least time you can give yourself should be sufficient enough to say سُبْحَانَ رَبِّيَ الْأَعْلَى three times, calmly and comfortably. Raising the forehead immediately after having rested it on the floor is prohibited.

In between the two Sajdahs:

1. Rising from the first *Sajdah,* sit up straight, on the hams, calmly and comfortably. Then go for the second *Sajdah.*

   Doing the second *Sajdah* after raising the head just a little bit and without becoming straight is a sin. If one does it like that, it becomes obligatory that the *Salaat* be made all over again.

2. Spread out the left foot (like the blade of a hockey stick) and sit on it. Let the right foot stand vertically with fingers turned towards the *Qiblah*. Some people let both feet remain in up right position and sit on the heels. This method is not correct.

3. While sitting, both hands should be placed on the thighs but fingers should not taper down onto the knees, instead, the far ends of the finger tips should reach only as far as the beginning edge of the knee.

4. While sitting, let your eyes be on the lap.

5. Sit for a time during which سُبْحَانَ اللهِ could be said at least once and if you can sit for a time during which اَللّٰهُمَّ اغْفِرْلِيْ وَارْحَمْنِيْ وَاهْدِنِيْ وَعَافِنِيْ وَارْزُقْنِيْ could be recited, it is better. But, reciting this during *Fard* (obligatory) *salah is not necessary. It is better to do so in Nafl Salah.*

The second Sajdah and rising from it :

1. Go on to do your second *Sajdah* in the same manner by first placing both hands on the floor, then the nose-tip, then the forehead .

2. The complete form of *Sajdah* should be the same as mentioned in connection with the first *Sajdah.*

3. When rising from *Sajdah,* first raise the forehead off the floor, then the nose-tip, then the hands, and then the knees.

4. While rising, it is better not to lean for support off the floor, however, should it be difficult to get up from the floor because of body-weight, sickness of old age, making use of the floor for support is also permissible.

5. After you have risen back to your standing position, recite بِسْمِ اللهِ الرَّحْمٰنِ الرَّحِيْمِ before *Surah al-Fatihah* in the beginning of each *rak'ah.*

In Qa'dah :

1. The method of sitting in *Qa'dah* shall be the same as mentioned in connection with the method of sitting between *Sajdahs*.

2. When you reach اَشْهَدُ اَنْ لَا اِلٰهَ اِلَّا اللّٰه while reciting raise الّتَحِيَّاتْ the *Shahadah* finger (the fore -finger or the index finger) with a pointing motion and let it fall back.

3. The method of making a pointing motion is that you make a circle by joining your middle finger and the thumb, close the little finger and the ring-finger (the one next to it), then raise the *shahadah* finger in a way that it is tapered towards in the *Qiblah*. It should not be raised up straight in   the direction of the sky.

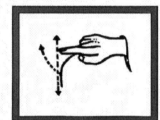

4. However, lower the *Shahadah* finger while saying اِلَّا اللّٰه but retain, right through the end, the initial formation of the rest of the fingers you already had when making the pointing motion.

When turning for Salam :

1. When turning for *Salam* on both sides, you should turn your neck just enough that your cheeks become visible to the person sitting behind you.

2. When turning for *Salam,* eyes should be towards the shoulders.

3. When turning your neck to the right to say السَّلَامُ عَلَيْكُمْ وَرَحْمَةُ اللّٰهِ make an intention that you are offering your *Salam* greetings to all human beings and angels on your right. Similarly, while turning for *Salam* to the left, have the intention of offering your *Salam* greetings to all human beings and angels present on your left.

First Right   **Then Left**

 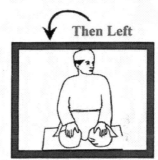

The method of Du'a:

1. The method of *Du'a* is that both hands be raised high enough so that they come in front of the chest. Let there be some space between the two hands. Do not bring the hands close together nor keep them far apart.

2. When making *Du'a*, keep the inner side of the hands turned towards your face.

Your opinion matters!

Hey!

Can I ask you for a favor? If you've read any of our books, could you please take 3 mins to post your honest review on Amazon? It doesn't have to be elaborate: Just share your thoughts about the book, if it helped you or not, if so, how.. stuff like that.

Rate This Book

Rate Your Experience With Seller
(The Islamic Quran Academy)

So every review means a lot to us.

To leave a review, just click the Book Buying link on Amazon.

Kind regards,
[The Islamic Quran Academy]

Made in the USA
Middletown, DE
17 September 2024

60960876R00033